Faithfulness

RESOURCES FOR BIBLICAL LIVING

Lou Priolo, series editor

Faithfulness

No More Excuses

LOU PRIOLO

P&R PUBLISHING
P.O. BOX 817 • PHILLIPSBURG • NEW JERSEY 08865-0817

Unless otherwise indicated, Scripture quotations are from the NEW AMERICAN STANDARD BIBLE®. Copyright © 1960, 1962, 1963, 1968, 1971, 1972, 1973, 1975, 1977, 1995 by The Lockman Foundation. Used by permission.

Scripture quotations marked (ESV) are from the ESV® Bible (The Holy Bible, English Standard Version®), copyright © 2001 by Crossway, a publishing ministry of Good News Publishers. Used by permission. All rights reserved.

Scripture quotations marked (NKJV) are from The Holy Bible, New King James Version. Copyright © 1979, 1980, 1982, Thomas Nelson, Inc.

Italics within Scripture quotations indicate emphasis added.

This booklet expands on material presented in the section "Faithfulness Is the Key" from *Keeping Your Cool: A Teen's Survival Guide* (Phillipsburg, NJ: P&R Publishing, 2014), 210–12.

ISBN: 978-1-62995-098-3 (pbk)
ISBN: 978-1-62995-099-0 (ePub)
ISBN: 978-1-62995-100-3 (Mobi)

Printed in the United States of America

PERHAPS YOU ARE THINKING, "Why was this booklet recommended to me? After all, I hardly ever miss devotions; I attend church twice a week; I always tell the truth (well, almost always); I even brush my teeth after every meal." May I suggest that if that is your attitude, you may need to read this booklet more than you realize. I say this because, as a general rule, the more faithful we become, the more we realize how *unfaithful* we have been. This should become more apparent in the pages ahead.

But for now I would like to draw your attention to the fact that this character trait is perhaps the most important quality required of us for Christian service. "Moreover, it is required of stewards that they be found faithful" (1 Cor. 4:2 ESV).[1] The development of this particular quality is so vital to ministry that I daresay if one does not seek to possess it, he will limit the number of important assignments given to him by Christian leaders (or by the Lord Himself for that matter). Whatever it is that you want to do for the Lord, be it in your local church (as a pastor, church officer,[2] missionary, Sunday school teacher, nursery worker, or member of the choir), in your vocation (as a doctor, nurse, CEO of a corporation, salesperson, business

[1]. The word for *steward* (*oikonos*) occurs ten times in the New Testament. Nine of the occurrences are in reference to an individual who has authority over subordinates. But in 1 Peter 4:10 (ESV), the word is used more broadly to apply to all believers: "As each one has received a gift, use it to serve one another, as good *stewards* of God's varied grace."

[2]. Although *faithfulness* is not specifically listed as a qualification for men who desire to be officers in either of the two New Testament passages that list such qualifications—1 Timothy 3 and Titus 1—the quality is implicit in both of those passages. The aforementioned word for *steward* (*oikonos*) is used. "For an overseer, as God's *steward*, must be above reproach. He must not be arrogant" (Titus 1:7 ESV). So, in light of 1 Corinthians 4:2, faithfulness may actually be an implicit qualification for elders.

owner, factory worker, home educator, or homemaker), or in your family, to be truly qualified for and successful in your endeavors, you must possess this quality.

So what comes to your mind when you hear the word *faithfulness*? How do you picture this important piece of the fruit of the Spirit?[3] This is a word that seems to involve so many things that it's difficult to grasp. But in reality it's quite simple to understand, as I trust you will shortly see.

Now, although it is simple to understand, faithfulness is sometimes difficult to develop—perhaps because it usually takes time to cultivate. So, before we unpack this term, let's take a brief look at the Lord's teaching on forgiveness, found in Luke 17:3–4. It will help to set the stage for our discussion of this character trait by helping us to see that becoming faithful is possible, even though it may seem rather challenging.

> Be on your guard! If your brother sins, rebuke him; and if he repents, forgive him. And if he sins against you seven times a day, and returns to you seven times, saying, "I repent," forgive him.

Jesus gave the disciples a pair of difficult injunctions. First He told them that they should rebuke (convict) those who sin against them. Then He instructed them to forgive their offenders as soon as they verbally expressed repentance over their sin.[4] He went on to explain that they were to forgive not just one occurrence of a sin but up to *seven occurrences in the same day.*

You may remember how incredulously the apostles responded to these orders. They said, (essentially), "You've got to be kidding!": "The apostles said to the Lord, 'Increase our faith!'" (Luke 17:5). The disciples thought that they needed more faith before they could do what the Lord had told them.

---

3. "But the fruit of the Spirit is love, joy, peace, patience, kindness, goodness, *faithfulness*, gentleness, self-control; against such things there is no law" (Gal. 5:22–23).

4. In other words, in the absence of evidence to the contrary, they were to take the offender at his word when he repented.

But Jesus explained to them that it wasn't more faith that they needed—it was more faithful obedience. They needed to do what they were expected to do by their Master regardless of how difficult it seemed, regardless of how they may have felt, regardless of how long it may have taken to accomplish the task.

> And the Lord said, "If you had faith like a mustard seed, you would say to this mulberry tree, 'Be uprooted and be planted in the sea'; and it would obey you. Which of you, having a slave plowing or tending sheep, will say to him when he has come in from the field, 'Come immediately and sit down to eat'? But will he not say to him, 'Prepare something for me to eat, and properly clothe yourself and serve me while I eat and drink; and afterward you may eat and drink'? He does not thank the slave because he did the things which were commanded, does he? So you too, when you do all the things which are commanded you, say, 'We are unworthy slaves; we have done only that which we ought to have done.'" (Luke 17:6–10)

As an old preacher–fishing buddy of mine likes to portray it,[5] imagine that you are just conversing with a brother (or sister) at church who is a new convert. You are not being provocative at all, just trying to engage him in conversation, when all of a sudden he bops you upside the head!

"Ouch! What are you doing?!" you ask.

He says to you, "Oh, I am so sorry! I don't know what just came over me, but something you said made me angry—anyway, I am *really* sorry for hurting you. Will you please forgive me?"

"Okay, I forgive you. But I don't feel like talking to you right now. In fact, I would appreciate it if you would stay away from me until my head stops throbbing."[6]

---

5. The unadulterated version of this illustration, as well as the inspiration for other material throughout this section, can be found in Jay E. Adams, *From Forgiven to Forgiving: Learning to Forgive One Another God's Way* (Amityville, NY: Calvary Press, 1994), 19–20.

6. Jesus says you have to forgive him; He didn't say you have to trust him.

Then five minutes later he sneaks up behind you, twirls you around, and hits you on the other side of your head.

"Ouch!!! I can't believe you did that again! You said you were sorry! Why did you hit me again?"

"Oh, I can't believe I did it either! I don't know what came over me. . . . Yes, I do—I was just thinking again about what you said, and my temper got the best of me and charged off to confront you before I realized what I was doing. I'm sooo sorry! If you will forgive me, I won't do it again and I will stay away from you. I promise!"

So you forgive him a second time. But suppose that before the day is over he manages to do it not just once, not twice, but seven times! Now after the second or third time you are going to begin to question his sincerity, right? But you know that there is not enough time to change bad habits in one day—especially, let's say, for a baby Christian. So according to Jesus you are going to have to take him at his word (preferring to believe the best rather than the worst)[7] if he says he is repentant, and you will have to grant him forgiveness. You will have to do (and, fortunately, you can *learn* to do) what Jesus said, even though it may seem hard or humanly impossible.

Who Can Find a Faithful Man?

Solomon asked in Proverbs 20:6, "Many a man proclaims his own loyalty, but who can find a trustworthy man?" Faithfulness has always been valued in biblical leaders. Old Testament saints like Moses (Heb. 3:5), Abraham (Neh. 9:8), David (1 Sam. 22:14), and Daniel (Dan. 6:4) were all said to be faithful. Nehemiah identified several of his workers as faithful (Neh. 7:2; 13:13). In the New Testament, the apostle Paul would identify some of his friends in the ministry as faithful. There was Timothy (1 Cor. 4:7), Epaphras (Col. 1:7), Tychicus (Eph. 6:21; Col. 4:7),

7. See 1 Corinthians 13:7.

Onesimus (Col. 4:9), and Sylvanus (1 Peter 5:12). But our greatest example of faithfulness in the Bible is that of our Lord and Savior Jesus Christ. Faithfulness is a fundamental element of His character.

> [He] was faithful to him who appointed him, just as Moses also was faithful in all God's house. . . . Moses was faithful in all God's house as a servant . . . but Christ is faithful over God's house as a son. (Heb. 3:2, 5, 6 ESV; see also 2:17)

Faithfulness is also a communicable[8] characteristic of God the Father (see Deut. 7:9; Pss. 36:5; 86:15; 89:8; 119:90; Lam. 3:22–23; 1 Cor. 1:9; 10:13). God is faithful and relates to His people by making and faithfully keeping His promises. "Faithfulness lies at the heart of the covenant relationship. God pledges constant fidelity to his promises, and this is why he expresses himself through covenants. God pledges a lasting relationship, and we are invited—indeed, called—to commit our lives with a commensurate faithfulness."[9]

People in leadership usually recognize the importance of faithfulness. King David was one of them. He says in Psalm 101, "My eyes shall be upon the faithful of the land, that they may dwell with me; he who walks in a blameless way is the one who will minister to me" (v. 6). He wanted faithful people in his court.

One summer, during my college years, I applied for a job. After landing the job I decided to ask how much it would pay. The boss said to me, "Lou, we are going to start you at $3.50 an hour, and after 30 days, if you do a real good job, we will let you keep it." My boss understood the concept of faithfulness. If you are an employer, you cannot afford to hire an unfaithful man or an unfaithful woman. Proverbs 25:19 (NKJV) warns,

8. I.e., one that can be communicated or transmitted to us.
9. Walter A. Elwell, ed., *Evangelical Dictionary of Theology* (Grand Rapids: Baker, 1984), 403.

"Confidence in an unfaithful man in time of trouble is like a broken tooth and a foot out of joint." You cannot depend upon, trust, or rely upon unfaithful people.

I also had a college professor who used to say the most interesting thing as he would hand out the syllabus at the beginning of every course: "Don't expect to get an A for this class if you simply fulfill the requirements on the syllabus. If you really want to get an A, you should aim at going above and beyond the call of duty."

Three Key Elements of Faithfulness

Next let's consider the parable of the talents found in Matthew 25. I would like to unpack three aspects of faithfulness—three elements that can be seen in this parable. Let's consider verse 14 first. "For [the kingdom of heaven] is just like a man about to go on a journey, who called his own slaves and *entrusted* his possessions to them." The Greek word in this context (*paradidomi*) means to entrust or commit—to give or assign someone a responsibility. The first thing you have to understand about faithfulness is that it involves the giving and accepting of *responsibility*.[10] God has entrusted you with a variety of specific responsibilities. The responsibilities may be in the form of gifts, abilities, or talents; of tasks or familial and vocational duties; or of ministries. "As each has received a gift, use it to serve one another, as good stewards of God's varied grace" (1 Peter 4:10 ESV). We all have responsibilities that have been assigned to us by God or indirectly by His agents.

Most of us have two types of responsibilities: those that we really enjoy doing and those that we don't enjoy doing. I don't know about you, but at the end of any given week, those responsibilities that I have neglected to do are usually the ones that

---

10. Or of a *stewardship*—"It is required of stewards that one be found trustworthy" (1 Cor. 4:2). Jesus, in this parable, is explaining to His disciples that they have been entrusted with certain God-given gifts of which they are required to be faithful stewards.

I didn't want to do in the first place. Yet somehow I manage to consistently fulfill those responsibilities that I enjoy doing. But a faithful Christian fulfills his duties whether he wants to do them (whether he feels like doing them) or not. An unfaithful person does what he feels like doing and doesn't do what he doesn't feel like doing.

"But when I don't feel like doing something and I do it anyway," you may object, "I feel like such a hypocrite! Is God really pleased with that kind of obedience?"

It depends on your motives. Obeying the Lord when you don't feel like doing so may be a greater manifestation of your love for Him than obeying when you are happy to do so. You see, it is not a matter of hypocrisy to feel one way and act another way—that is a matter of responsibility. It is hypocrisy to profess one thing and do another. If you were to say to God or to another person, "I just loved doing that responsibility," even though you really didn't, that would be hypocrisy.

Take a moment right now and record your top daily or weekly responsibilities.

What Are My Top Ten God-Given Responsibilities?

1. _____
2. _____
3. _____
4. _____
5. _____
6. _____
7. _____
8. _____
9. _____
10. _____

Now place each of these responsibilities into one of the following categories.

Responsibilities I Want to Fulfill	Responsibilities I Don't Want to Fulfill
1. _____	1. _____
2. _____	2. _____
3. _____	3. _____
4. _____	4. _____
5. _____	5. _____
6. _____	6. _____
7. _____	7. _____
8. _____	8. _____
9. _____	9. _____
10. _____	10. _____

Someone has defined the characteristic of being responsible this way: "knowing and doing what God and others are expecting of me."[11] Do you know what God and others expect of you? With what stewardships have you been entrusted? What responsibilities do you have right now? Do you see any of these as your divinely delegated duties? Some examples are below.

☐ To grow by grace (to use the means of grace that God has provided for your spiritual growth)
☐ To be the loving leader of your home
☐ To provide for your family's needs
☐ To be a helper to your husband
☐ To teach your children God's Word
☐ To honor and obey your parents

11. This definition of *responsibility* is from the Institute in Basic Life Principles "Character Bookshelf Series" game entitled Character Clues (Oak Brook, IL: Institute in Basic Youth Conflicts, 1974).

- ☐ To study and do your homework
- ☐ To be a faithful employee or employer at work
- ☐ To actively participate in your local church
- ☐ To serve others in ministry
- ☐ To balance your checkbook (or at least to be sure you don't spend more than you take in)
- ☐ To keep the possessions entrusted to you in good repair
- ☐ To proclaim the good news about Jesus Christ to those who haven't heard it

Let's look next at verse 15 of Matthew 25. "To one he gave five talents, to another, two, and to another, one, each according to his own ability; and he went on his journey." It is not so much our ability that counts (because God has given each of us gifts and talents, as the text says, according to our abilities; see Rom. 12:3–8; James 1:17).[12] Rather, it is more what we *do* with these God-given abilities that matters in God's economy.

> Immediately the one who had received the five talents went and traded with them, and gained five more talents. In the same manner the one who had received the two talents gained two more. But he who received the one talent went away, and dug a hole in the ground and hid his master's money. Now after a long time the master of those slaves came and *settled accounts* with them. (Matt. 25:16–19)

The words in italics above disclose the second building block of faithfulness. It is the principle of *accountability*. The King James Version renders the phrase "settle accounts with them" (Greek: *sunario* + *logos*) as "reckoneth with them." You and I will be held accountable for faithfully fulfilling the responsibilities that God has entrusted to us. This same phrase is also translated in Matthew 18:23 (the parable of the unforgiving servant) as

12. Also, in 1 Corinthians 4:7, Paul asks, "What do you have that you did not receive?" ("Nothing" is the expected answer.) "And if you did receive it, why do you boast as if you had not received it?"

"settling accounts": "For this reason the kingdom of heaven may be compared to a king who wished to settle accounts with his slaves."

The fact is that we are all accountable to someone. The people I counsel are, at some level, accountable to me, as are the members of my immediate family. I am accountable to the elders of my church. The Session (elder board) of my church is accountable at one level to our congregation, and at another level to our presbytery (the governing body of ministers in our geographic area). And in some areas of life, of course, we are accountable only to God, as Paul said in Romans 14:12—"Each one of us will give an account of himself to God."

Now, one of the most important things about principle number two is that without it, there could be no principle number three. And principle number three is arguably the best of the three principles. It is the principle of *rewards*.

You and I will be rewarded according to our faithfulness or according to our unfaithfulness.

> The one who had received the five talents came up and brought five more talents, saying, "Master, you entrusted five talents to me. See, I have gained five more talents." (Matt. 25:20)

Here comes the reward.

> His master said to him, "Well done, good and faithful slave." (v. 21)

He gets commended.

> "You were faithful with a few things, I will put you in charge of many things; enter into the joy of your master." Also the one who had received the two talents came up and said, "Master, you entrusted two talents to me. See, I have gained two more talents." His master said to him, "Well done, good and faithful slave. You were faithful with a few things, I will put you in charge of many things; enter into the joy of your master." (vv. 21–22)

Goodness has to do with what I am, including my motives. Faithfulness has to do with what I do, assuming that my motives are right. So the master says, "Well done, good and faithful servant." Part of our reward is commendation, but there is another part. A much more important part of our reward, when we execute our responsibilities faithfully—and really even if we don't—has to do with whether or not we are granted additional responsibilities.

Now, if you don't get anything else from this booklet, please make sure that you understand this: Faithfulness results in our receiving a future reward based on our fulfillment of past responsibilities. If you faithfully fulfill the responsibilities that God has given you today, you will be honored at some point in the future—not only will you receive commendation, but you will be rewarded with *additional responsibilities*.[13] And that begins the next phase of the process—the next step up the ladder.

If you don't faithfully fulfill the responsibilities you have been given, you will not be entrusted or rewarded with greater responsibilities. You see, there is a negative side of this principle as well. Look carefully at verses 24–30.

> The one also who had received the one talent came up and said, "Master, I knew you to be a hard man, reaping where you did not sow and gathering where you scattered no seed. And I was afraid, and went away and hid your talent in the ground. See, you have what is yours." But his master answered and said to him, "You wicked, lazy slave, you knew that I reap where I did not sow and gather where I scattered no seed. Then you ought to have put my money in the bank, and on my arrival I would have received my money back with interest. Therefore take away the talent from him, and give it to the one who has the ten talents." For to everyone who has, more shall be given, and he will have an abundance; but from the one who does

13. The Greek word for "put you in charge" in verses 21 and 23 (*katasteso*; "I will *put you in charge* of many things") means "to set in an elevated position, in an office."

not have, even what he does have shall be taken away. Throw out the worthless slave into the outer darkness; in that place there will be weeping and gnashing of teeth.

The unfaithful slave received condemnation rather than commendation. Instead of his being given additional responsibilities, the few responsibilities that he had were taken from him (Greek: *airo*, "to remove from"). So there is a reward for unfaithfulness too—the wages of unfaithfulness is the loss of responsibility.

Below is a diagram I often use (usually by drawing it on a whiteboard) to make it easier for those whom I counsel to better understand and remember the concept of faithfulness.

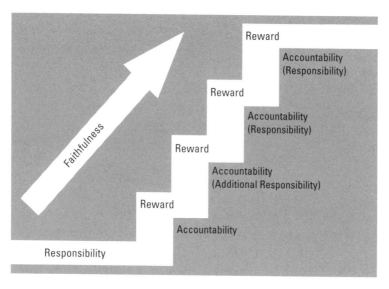

So here is a definition of faithfulness extrapolated from the aforementioned passages: faithfulness is demonstrating to God and others that I can be trusted with more and more responsibilities based on my past performance.[14] As Jesus said, "Everyone to whom much was given, of him much will be required, and

14. By *performance* I mean the *manner* (whether faithful or unfaithful) in which my entrusted responsibilities were executed.

from him to whom they entrusted much, they will demand the more" (Luke 12:48 ESV).

"But what does it mean to be faithful in plain English? Can you give me a synonym for it?"

Sure! It's very simple. If you are faithful, it means that you are *trustworthy*. It means that you are *dependable*. It means that you are *reliable*. As a rule, whenever you see the word *faithfulness* in the Scriptures, you can substitute any one of those synonyms and you will get a pretty good picture of what the word entails.

Incidentally, this principle has much relevance to how a Christian leader should be treated when he has had some kind of a fall into sin. There are typically two extreme attitudes (postures) that churches tend to adopt when someone who is in a position of Christian leadership falls. One extreme is "He is through. Get rid of him—the sooner the better. He will never be in any kind of ministry again." The other unbiblical extreme is along these lines: "Let's set him on the sideline for a couple of years. 'Hush hush' the thing, and maybe in a few years we will put him back at the same level from which he fell."

That is not the way it is supposed to work. How did that missionary, or seminary president, or whoever it is get to the point from which he fell? Did he just walk out of college or out of high school and apply for the job? No. He had to start at the bottom. After high school, he went to college. Maybe when he was in college he did what I did and sold shoes or was a nurse's aide in a neonatal section of a local hospital—something far different, far less prestigious perhaps, than where he ended up. But he was entrusted with a set of responsibilities. He was held accountable and he was rewarded for faithfully executing those responsibilities, and part of that reward was another set of responsibilities. Then there was more accountability, and then he was rewarded with more responsibility. Rung by rung, step by step by step, he got to the top of the ladder. When we stumble, that is the way that the restoration process (generally speaking) should proceed. We go back to one of the lower rungs of the ladder (probably not all the way to the first rung), but at some point we have to demonstrate to those around us that we are faithful again (see 1 Tim. 3:10). We will have to re-climb a portion of the ladder before we can be fully restored.[15]

We can find these three elements or principles of faithfulness in another passage of Scripture. In 1 Corinthians 3:10, Paul is attempting to deal with the carnality of some in Corinth who seemed to be following certain men rather than, or at least more than, Christ. "According to the grace of God which was given to me, like a wise master builder I laid a foundation, and another is building on it."

Paul was sort of like a contractor who specialized in pouring concrete. He would go into a city, scope out the territory, design a blueprint for a local church based on the specs that he got from his Boss, lay the foundation, and then turn the rest of the building over to other faithful men. "The things which you have heard from me in the presence of many witnesses, entrust these to faithful men who will be able to teach others also" (2 Tim. 2:2). In this case it was pastors and teachers and evangelists. He laid the foundation, turned the job over to these other fellows—the subcontractors,[16] if you please—and then moved on to the next town.

Here is responsibility, the first principle of faithfulness: "But each man must be careful how he builds on it" (1 Cor. 3:10). Paul is going from his own personal experience to that of his readers. He is saying, "I do this in the context of the church," and then he is exhorting his readers to imitate his example of faithfulness.

15. Of course, some falls are so scandalous that the fallen minister or Christian worker may never be restored to the same level of ministry from which he fell. Regrettably, there may sometimes be no conceivable way for a fallen leader to ever be considered *above reproach* again (see 1 Tim. 3:2; Titus 1:6–7).

16. And by the way, if you ever want to verify the truthfulness of Proverbs 20:6 ("Who can find a trustworthy man?"), ask a general contractor. Who can find a faithful construction worker? I have it on good authority that it is very difficult these days.

He says, "each of you," and then later on he says, "any man," over and over again. He is saying in essence, "There is a bigger principle here. *Each of you* is building his own building. Christ is building His church of His people, but with His strength you are building a life that is meant to bring honor and glory to Christ. It is your responsibility to build your life on the foundation of Christ because He is *the* Foundation. He is the only foundation, 'for no man can lay a foundation other than the one which is laid, which is Jesus Christ' (1 Cor. 3:11)."

Paul wanted to be sure that the foundation was laid correctly, because he knew that the whole structure depended on it. So he personally oversaw its construction. But once the foundation was laid, he found other faithful workers and assigned them the responsibility of finishing the project. And *you* are one of those workers! You have been given the responsibility of helping to build Christ's church.[17] You have been given the responsibility of constructing a life that will bring honor and glory to Him. "Now if any man builds on the foundation with gold, silver, precious stones, wood, hay, straw, each man's work will become evident"—here comes principle number two: the principle of accountability—"for the day will show it because it is to be revealed with fire, and the fire itself will test the quality of each man's work" (1 Cor. 3:12–13). Someday, you and I will give an account of the manner in which we constructed our building. Did we use precious materials that could withstand the fire? What were our motives? How did we conduct ourselves on the job? How faithfully did we serve?

Now here is our final principle. "If any man's work which he has built on it remains, he will receive *a reward*" (v. 14). The New Testament speaks often of the rewards that we will receive in heaven. One of the most common ways it describes these rewards is as crowns (crowns of righteousness, crowns of life, crowns of exaltation, and crowns of glory). But we will be

---

17. You are actually a part of the building itself.

rewarded when we get to heaven for the way we built Christ's church and the way we conducted and constructed our lives down here. "If any man's work is burned up, he will suffer loss; but he himself will be saved, yet so as through fire" (v. 15). There is a negative reward—not the loss of eternal life, but the loss of some portion of your heavenly reward.[18] Your reward in heaven will correspond to the quality of material that you are using right now to complete your building.

The Greatest Obstacle to Faithfulness

Have you ever considered what the opposite of faithfulness is? Let's go back to Matthew 25 and take another look at verses 24–26, because this passage tells us the answer. See if you can't figure it out.

> And the one also who had received the one talent came up and said, "Master, I knew you to be a hard man, reaping where you did not sow and gathering where you scattered no seed. And I was afraid, and went away and hid your talent in the ground. See, you have what is yours." But his master answered and said to him, "You wicked, *lazy* slave."

The first two slaves were told that they were good and faithful. The third slave was told something entirely different. What is the opposite of being good?

"Is it being wicked?"

Exactly. What is the opposite of being faithful?

"That must be being lazy!"

Right again! "You wicked, lazy slave," his master says, "you knew that I reaped where I did not sow and gathered where I scattered no seed."

18. See also 2 John 8: "Watch yourselves, so that you may not lose what we have worked for, but may win a full reward" (ESV).

Laziness is not the only thing, but it is probably the principal thing that keeps most people from being faithful. And one of the chief characteristics of a lazy person is that he is full of excuses. "I knew you to be a hard man, reaping where you did not sow and gathering where you scattered no seed. And I was afraid, and went away and hid your talent in the ground" (vv. 24–25). Solomon put it this way: "The sluggard says, 'There is a lion outside; I will be killed in the streets!'" (Prov. 22:13).

Excuses, of course, began in the garden of Eden ("The woman you gave me, she gave me fruit and I did eat"; see Gen. 3:12), and they continue until this day. As a counselor, I have to deal with excuses regularly. One of the biggest, most important parts of a counselor's job is to disabuse people of their excuses. And, as you know, we get them all the time. Perhaps the most popular one I hear is, "I can't."

"I can't forgive him."

"I can't go back to my wife."

"I can't stop that habit."

"I can't do this and I can't do that."

My typical response to such excuses is, "You can't say 'can't' as a Christian." Then I quote Philippians 4:13: "I can do all things through Him who strengthens me." And I continue, "If God says that you must do it, you can't say 'can't.' As Christians, we can learn to do anything that the Bible says we should do."

"Well, you can't teach an old dog new tricks."

"I don't know much about dogs," I may reply. "I am not a dog trainer. It may be true about dogs, but God says over and over again that it is not true for people. You can and must change if you are a Christian, at any age."

"But that is just the way I am."

"Well, you will just have to be different, won't you?"

"You don't know what it's like to live with a husband like mine!"

"That may be true, but I do know what the Bible says about your response to a husband like yours. I may not know what it is like to have done this or done that or to have been married to such and such a person. But all I essentially have to know is what the Bible says about how a Christian should glorify God in any given set of circumstances. After all, some of the best obstetricians in the world are men." (Think about the implications of that one.)

And then there is the "I know, but" genre of excuses.

"I know what the Bible says, but . . ."

"I know I shouldn't speed, but I just put twin turbochargers on my new Jaguar."

"I know it is wrong to overeat, but if I don't eat it, it will go to waste."[19]

"I know I should control my temper, but my wife doesn't seem to understand anything else but screaming and yelling."

"I know I should obey my parents, but they are out of touch with reality."

"I know I shouldn't miss church, but the television evangelist holds my interest better my pastor does."

"I know I shouldn't be late for class, but I squeezed the toothpaste too hard and had a very difficult time getting it back into the tube."

"I know, but, but, but, but . . ." I once heard a preacher refer to such people as "Billy Goat Christians." What excuse-making Christians are really saying is, "Please excuse me from living a responsible (biblical) life on the basis that my case is different."

But God says that our cases are not different, and a faithful person realizes that. "No temptation has overtaken you but such as is common to man; and God is faithful [now you know what this word means], who will not allow you to be tempted beyond what you are able, but with the temptation will provide the way of escape also, so that you will be able to endure it" (1 Cor. 10:13).

---

19. It will go to waste one way or the other. If to waste food is a sin, to waste it by means of gluttony is a double sin.

What excuses have you used most often to justify neglecting your responsibilities? Consider the following categories as you record them in the space provided below.

- ☐ "I can't" excuses (claiming not to have the ability to do what the Bible says you should do)
- ☐ Blame-shifting excuses ("I would have done that if so and so or such and such hadn't . . .")
- ☐ Family excuses ("My wife, husband, children, or parents kept me from . . .")
- ☐ Business/work-related excuses
- ☐ Possession excuses (the enjoyment or maintenance of that which you possess)
- ☐ Pleasure excuses (recreational things you would rather do than fulfill your responsibilities)

_____

_____

_____

_____

_____

_____

_____

_____

Fear and Excuses

Another characteristic of a lazy (and often of an unfaithful) person is that he is fearful. There is in the Bible a correlation between making excuses and being afraid.

I knew you to be a hard man, reaping where you did not sow and gathering where you scattered no seed. And I was afraid, and went away and hid your talent in the ground. (Matt. 25:24–25)

23

They heard the sound of the LORD God walking in the garden in the cool of the day, and the man and his wife *hid themselves* from the presence of the LORD God among the trees of the garden. Then the LORD God called to the man, and said to him, "Where are you?" He said, "I heard the sound of You in the garden, and *I was afraid* because I was naked; so I hid myself." And He said, "Who told you that you were naked? Have you eaten from the tree of which I commanded you not to eat?" The man said, "*The woman whom You gave to be with me, she gave me from the tree, and I ate.*" (Gen. 3:8–12)

But some days later Felix arrived with Drusilla, his wife who was a Jewess, and sent for Paul and heard him speak about faith in Christ Jesus. But as he was discussing righteousness, self-control and the judgment to come, Felix became *frightened* and said, "Go away for the present, and *when I find time I will summon you.*" (Acts 24:24–25)

Fear is a powerful emotion that often paralyzes those who do not know how to handle it biblically. When we allow fear and worry to take a foothold, our minds become so consumed by them that we become distracted from focusing our attention on our responsibilities. So we neglect them because we are, to varying degrees, crippled by our anxious thoughts. Consequently we succumb (at least temporarily) to laziness and/or unfaithfulness. What specific fears have kept you from fulfilling your biblical responsibilities?

☐ Fear of rejection
☐ Fear of conflict
☐ Fear of failure
☐ Fear of embarrassment
☐ Fear of punishment
☐ Fear of loneliness
☐ Fear of losing control
☐ Fear of poverty
☐ Fear of boredom
☐ Fear of dying
☐ Fear of pain
☐ Fear of losing freedom
☐ Fear of being less than perfect
☐ Fear of speaking improperly

- ☐ Fear of proper consequences
- ☐ Fear of improper consequences (i.e., consequences that we imagine, even if they are unrealistic and unlikely to actually happen)
- ☐ Fear of litigation
- ☐ Fear of the unknown
- ☐ Fear of getting angry
- ☐ Fear of traveling
- ☐ Fear of something bad happening to a loved one
- ☐ Other: _____
- ☐ Other: _____

Three Tests of a Faithful Person

Let's consider next the three tests of a faithful man or woman. The tests are found after the parable of the unjust steward in Luke 16. Incidentally, you can find the three principles of faithfulness in this passage also. The unjust steward was given a *responsibility*—a stewardship. He was held *accountable*: "Give an account of your stewardship" (v. 2 NKJV). He was *rewarded* for his unfaithful practices by losing his stewardship. Check it out on your own.

So what are the three tests of a faithful man or woman?[20] First, a faithful man or woman is *faithful in little things*. "He who is faithful in a very little thing is faithful also in much; and he who is unrighteous in a very little thing is unrighteous also in much" (v. 10). Little things are important. How faithful are you with the little things? Little things like the promises that you made, the ministries that you have assumed, the thank-you notes that are weeks overdue. Little things like keeping the car clean, returning telephone calls, doing household repairs, responding to those e-mails that you really didn't want to receive in the first place.[21] Little things like reading the directions on something before

20. Years ago, in Bible college, I heard a sermon by Melvin Upchurch in which he unpacked this passage. Material in this section was influenced by that sermon.

21. Now, I haven't found it yet, but I know that somewhere in Scripture there must be an exception to the faithfulness rule when it comes to responding to unsolicited e-mail.

you try to assemble it. Little things like using good grammar and practicing good table manners.[22]

Little things are important to God. Which little things are you most likely to let slip? How often do you typically neglect them? Record your answers below.

Responsibilities I am most likely to let slip	Frequency with which I neglect them
	_____ times per day/week/month
	_____ times per day/week/month
	_____ times per day/week/month
	_____ times per day/week/month
	_____ times per day/week/month
	_____ times per day/week/month
	_____ times per day/week/month

The second test of a faithful man or woman is *faithfulness in finances*. "Therefore if you have not been faithful in the use of unrighteous wealth, who will entrust the true riches to you?" (Luke 16:11). The word *riches* is not in the original. "If therefore you have not been faithful in the use of your money," Jesus says, "who will commit *the truth* to you?" If you don't handle your finances right, you are going to have a difficult time applying the Bible to your life.

How I Handle Money	How I Handle the Truth
Do I view money as a stewardship entrusted to me by God? (Do I see God as the source of my wealth?)	Do I see the truth as a stewardship committed to me by God? (Do I see God as the source of truth?)

22. Of course things like not having good grammar or table manners are not sins per se. But not doing those little things that people in positions of authority have instructed us to do often constitute sins of omission.

Do I use my money primarily for my own selfish purposes or for God's glory and the benefit of others?	Do I use my wisdom for selfish purposes (i.e., to make people think well of me) or for God's glory and the benefit of others?
Do I give God's money for the cause of Christ, or do I hoard it?	Do I share God's Word for the cause of Christ, or do I hoard it (keep it to myself)?
To what degree am I concerned about feeding the poor?	To what degree am I concerned about feeding the spiritually poor (and immature)?
Do I save some of my earnings for future use?	Do I hide Scripture in my heart for future use?
Am I laying up treasure on earth?	Am I laying up treasure in heaven?
Am I honest in all my financial dealings?	Am I honest in the interpretation and application of Scripture?
Do I work hard for my money (rather than depending on others to provide for my sustenance, with little or no effort of my own)?	Do I work hard to understand the Bible (to feed myself, rather than depending only on others to feed me spiritually)?
Do I throw money away on things I don't need?	Do I cast my pearls before swine?
Am I prone to follow "get rich quick" schemes?	Am I prone to follow "instant" or easy methods of spiritual sanctification?
How many days per week do I spend earning money?	How many days per week do I spend reading, studying, or memorizing God's Word?
Do I keep track of (keep records of) my finances?	Do I keep track of (keep records of) what the Lord has taught me through His Word?
Do I love money more than I love the truth and wisdom? (Do I long to be more financially prosperous than spiritually prosperous?)	Do I love the truth and wisdom more than I love money? (Do I long to be more spiritually prosperous than financially prosperous?)
Do I plan to teach my children how to provide for themselves when I am gone? (Am I planning to leave an inheritance to my children?)	Do I plan to teach my children how to provide for themselves spiritually when I am gone? (Am I planning to leave a spiritual inheritance to my children?)

The third test of a faithful man or woman is faithfulness in that which is another's. "If you have not been faithful in the use of that which is another's, who will give you that which is your own?" (Luke 16:12). Stewardship involves the management of another person's goods. A steward is one who is entrusted with the management of property, finances, or other affairs that are not his own.

Whose affairs are you managing?	What are they?
☐ God's	_____
	_____
	_____
	_____
	_____
☐ Your employer's	_____
	_____
	_____
	_____
	_____
☐ Your spouse's	_____
	_____
	_____
	_____
	_____
☐ Your parents'	_____
	_____
	_____
	_____
	_____

☐ Your _____   _____

                                _____

                                _____

                                _____

                                _____

I had a professor whose personal policy was never to borrow anything without giving it back in better condition. He might paint it or clean it or fix it somehow, but he wouldn't give it back to the person from whom he had borrowed it until it was in better condition than when he picked it up.

Have you ever considered the fact that Jesus borrowed a lot of things? He borrowed a manger, He borrowed food (remember the fish and the bread?), He borrowed boats and cups, He borrowed a colt and an upper room. He even borrowed a tomb. And you can be sure that He returned those things in proper condition.

Do you have a clearer understanding of what it means to be faithful than you did when you began this booklet? I trust that you do. To review, first there is a working definition of faithfulness: "demonstrating to God and others that I can be trusted with greater and greater responsibilities based on the faithful execution of my former responsibilities." Then there are the three principles of faithfulness: responsibility, accountability, and rewards. And lastly the synonyms for faithfulness: dependability, reliability, and trustworthiness. This is the kind of person who I look for when I am hiring a new staff member at our counseling center. This is the kind of person whom God is looking to put into His service. As Paul told Timothy, "I thank Christ Jesus our Lord, who has strengthened me, because He considered me faithful, putting me into service" (1 Tim. 1:12).

Appendix:
Two Types of Stewards

The chart below shows the contrast between stewards (managers) who are faithful and those who are not. Now that you have finished this booklet, why not take a moment to open your Bible and review each descriptive phrase in its biblical context?

The Slothful Steward	The Faithful Steward
"As vinegar to the teeth and smoke to the eyes, so is the lazy one to those who send him." (Prov. 10:26)	"Like the cold of snow in the time of harvest is a faithful messenger to those who send him." (Prov. 25:13)
☐ is an expert at making excuses (Prov. 22:13)	☐ will not make excuses (Prov. 14:5)
☐ does not take care of personal possessions (Prov. 24:30–31)	☐ takes good care of others' possessions (Luke 16:12)
☐ refuses responsibility (Prov. 21:25)	☐ is entrusted with additional responsibility (2 Tim. 2:2)
☐ does only what he wants to do (Prov. 21:25)	☐ does what he is supposed to do (1 Cor. 4:2)
☐ tends to be a busybody (2 Thess. 3:11)	☐ can keep a secret (Prov. 11:13)
☐ will likely end up in poverty (Prov. 6:9–11)	☐ will abound in blessing (Prov. 28:20)